American Institute of Homeopathy

Program of Section

American Institute of Homeopathy

Program of Section

ISBN/EAN: 9783337255671

Printed in Europe, USA, Canada, Australia, Japan

Cover: Foto ©Andreas Hilbeck / pixelio.de

More available books at **www.hansebooks.com**

1844—1894

SEMI-CENTENNIAL

THE

American Institute of Homoeopathy

DENVER

SECTION OF

Materia Medica and General Therapeutics

FRANK KRAFT, M.D., Cleveland, *Chairman.*
WM. E. LEONARD, M.D., Minneapolis, *Secretary.*

PROGRAM OF SECTION

Contributors to the Section of Materia Medica and Therapeutics

R. E. DUDGEON, M.D., London.

RICHARD HUGHES, M.D., Brighton.

THOS. SKINNER, M.D., London.

EDWARD T. BLAKE, M.D., London.

JOHN W. HAYWARD, M.D., Birkenhead. P. JOUSSET, M.D., Paris.

CARL BOJANUS, Sr., M.D., Samara, Russia.

COLLEGES.*

CHAS. MOHR, M.D., Prof. Materia Medica and Therapeutics, *Hahnemann Medical College and Hospital* (Philadelphia).

PEMBERTON DUDLEY, M.D., Prof. Institutes of Medicine and Hygiene, *Hahnemann Medical College and Hospital* (Philadelphia).

W. B. HINSDALE, M.D., Prof. Philosophical and Applied Materia Medica and Organon and Clinical Therapeutics, *Cleveland University of Medicine and Surgery* (Cleveland).

L. C. MCELWEE, M.D., Prof. of Drug Pathogenesy, and Co-Professor of Materia Medica and Therapeutics, *Homœopathic Medical College of Missouri* (St. Louis).

J. E. GILMAN, M.D., Prof. of Materia Medica, Therapeutics and Institutes, *Hahnemann Medical College and Hospital* (Chicago).

T. F. ALLEN, M.D., Prof. of Materia Medica and Therapeutics, *New York Homœopathic Medical College and Hospital* (New York).

---

* Arranged according to age of College.

A. R. McMichael, M.D., Prof. of Materia Medica and Therapeutics, *New York Medical College and Hospital for Women* (New York).

Henry Snow, M.D., Prof. Materia Medica and Therapeutics, *Pulte Medical College* (Cincinnati).

J. Heber Smith, M.D., Prof. Materia Medica, *Boston University School of Medicine* (Boston).

Conrad Wesselhœft, M.D., Prof. Pathology and Therapeutics, *Boston University School of Medicine* (Boston).

Chas. S. Mack, M.D., Prof. Materia Medica and Therapeutics, *Homœopathic Medical Department University of Michigan* (Ann Arbor).

A. W. Woodward, M.D., Prof. Materia Medica and Therapeutics, *Chicago Homœopathic Medical College* (Chicago).

A. C. Cowperthwaite, M.D., Prof. Materia Medica and Therapeutics, *Chicago Homœopathic Medical College* (Chicago).

Geo. Royal, M.D., Prof. Materia Medica and Therapeutics, *Homœopathic Department of Iowa State University* (Iowa City).

William Bœricke, M.D., Prof. Materia Medica and Therapeutics, *Hahnemann Hospital College* (SanFrancisco).

W. A. Dewey, M.D., Late Prof. Materia Medica and Therapeutics, *Hahnemann Hospital College* (SanFrancisco).

W. E. Leonard, M.D., Prof. Materia Medica and Therapeutics, *Homœopathic Department of State University of Minnesota* (Minneapolis).

Mark Edgerton, M.D., Prof. of Materia Medica and Therapeutics, *Kansas City Homœopathic Medical College* (Kansas City).

Eldridge C. Price, M.D., Prof. Materia Medica and Therapeutics, *Southern Homœopathic Medical College* (Baltimore).

W. O. CHEESEMAN, M.D., Prof. Materia Medica and Clinical Therapeutics, *National Homœopathic Medical College* (Chicago).

W. J. HAWKES, M D., Prof. of Materia Medica and Clinical Therapeutics, *Hering Medical College and Hospital* (Chicago).

H. C. ALLEN, M.D., Prof. Materia Medica and Organon, *Hering Medical College and Hospital* (Chicago).

A. LEIGHT MONROE, M D.,Prof. Materia Medica, and Lecturer on Orificial Surgery, *Southwestern Homœopathic Medical College* (Louisville).

OTHER CONTRIBUTORS.

JABEZ P. DAKE, M.D., Louisville.	HOWARD CRUTCHER, M.D., Chicago.
S. F. SHANNON, M.D., Denver.	T. C. DUNCAN, M.D., Chicago.
WILSON A. SMITH, M.D., Chicago.	FRANK KRAFT, M.D., Cleveland.
GEO. ROYAL, M.D., DesMoines.	G. E. GRAMM, M.D., Ardmore, PA.
GEO. B. PECK, M.D., Providence.	SAMUEL A. JONES, M.D., Ann Arbor.

SECTION 6.—In all discussions no speaker shall be allowed more than five minutes, nor to speak more than once upon the same subject, except by vote of consent taken in the usual manner.—*By-Laws.*

American Institute of Homœopathy.

Section of Materia Medica and General Therapeutics. 1893 and 1894.

First Baptist Church, Denver,
Friday, June 15th, 1894, 10 A.M.
Tuesday, June 19th, 1894, 10 A.M.

Order of Exercises.

Call to order.

Address of the Chairman, Dr. Frank Kraft, Cleveland.

STATEMENT.

The topic selected for the study and labors of this Section is

How to Teach, and How to Learn Materia Medica.

In order to reach these points in a systematic way and bring them prominently yet tersely before the profession of Homœopathic medicine, a series of questions was prepared and sent to the several teachers in our American homœopathic medical colleges, and as well to others at home and abroad not now engaged in teaching. In addition there have been many letters written to members eminent in the profession, and frequent notices have been placed in contemporary homœopathic medical journals: all soliciting reports and answers to these questions, in order that the present session of the Institute might indeed prove to be a materia medica session, and result in a *renaissance* of homœopathic teaching.

To these letters and invitations the Section has received responses from every college in the land, giving the methods of teaching; also full and graphic papers from our famous and ever popular English brethren: Drs. R. E. Dudgeon, Richard Hughes, Edward T. Blake, Thos. Skinner, and John T. Hayward; and a paper from Dr. P. Jousset, of Paris.

The mass of manuscript received in answer to these questions is altogether too large to print in this Order of Exercises, and is equally too ponderous to present in full at this session of the Institute. In order, however, to derive value from the ideas communicated by our brethren at home and abroad on this important subject, it is suggested that the papers of our Honorary members, Drs. Dudgeon and Hughes, be read in full, as they are more in the nature of essays of great merit than of simple statistical contributions, and that the remainder of the papers relating to this subject be read by synopsis as published in this Order of Exercises. Provided always that any paper may be called for by any member and read in part or in whole at the pleasure of the Section; the entire purpose being to present our subject in the best possible manner, that it may be fully and satisfactorily discussed, in the hope that out of this Sectional meeting may be evolved some uniform, if not more progressive way of teaching Materia Medica in our colleges.

It must not be understood, however, that the whole Section is devoted to the discussion of a subject which seems to be restricted to the teaching-corps. At a later hour in the Section's sittings papers of general Materia Medica interest will be presented in which all Institute members, whether in college or out, will find matter of interest and value. The title and synopsis of these papers will be found following the synopsis of answers to the Sectional question.

The general Sectional Topic, "HOW TO TEACH, AND HOW TO LEARN MATERIA MEDICA," was divided into the following five questions:

I. What advice do you give concerning Materia Medica to a student beginning medicine by a years' preliminary study?

II. What is the best method of teaching Materia Medica: (a) for the preceptor to his student; (b) for the teacher to his classes in the college; (c) give an outline of your method of teaching a drug in the class-room?

III.   Which is the best place for teaching Therapeutics—(1) Hospital; (2) Dispensary; (3) Clinic; (4) Class-room; or (5) Bedside; and how should it be done?

IV.   Do you teach the potency of the remedy studied? If not, why not? If you do, how do you explain the potency you advocate?

V.   When should the *Organon* be taught and how?

Prof. TIMOTHY FIELD ALLEN, of the *New York Homœopathic Medical College and Hospital*, New York, will open the Section by giving an address entitled:

An Introduction to the Study of the Salts of Potash.

As this will be practically a sample of lecture as delivered in the *New York Homœopathic College and Hospital*, it will be in line with the Sectional topic.

Discussion will be led by Dr. JABEZ P. DAKE, of Nashville.

How to Teach Materia Medica.

By R. E. DUDGEON, M.D., of London.

On the Best Methods of Studying and Teaching Materia Medica.

By RICHARD HUGHES, M.D., Brighton.

Method of Teaching Materia Medica.

By P. JOUSSET, M.D., of Paris.

Question 1.

What advice do you give concerning Materia Medica to a student beginning medicine by a year's preliminary study.

Answers.

Dr. R. E. DUDGEON, (*Honorary Member, London.*) – I have never had occasion to advise a student concerning the Materia Medica, and should think that, during his year's preliminary study, he had best give his whole attention to the subjects required for this preliminary study, and leave Materia Medica alone until he has mastered them.

Dr. RICHARD HUGHES, (*Honorary Member, Brighton.*)—On this point I should urge one thing, that the text-book commended to such a learner shall not be one consisting of symptom-lists. Of whatever use these may be to the practitioner, to a beginner they are uninteresting, confusing, disheartening. He wants an introduction which shall lead him by easy steps to the inner shrine. A literary work is required, one susceptible of continuous and not disagreeable reading; one that deals with outlines and generalities instead of burdening the memory with details. It was to supply such need mainly that I originally wrote my "*Pharmacodynamics.*" Prepare your student to approach with zest his further studies in this sphere.

Wm. E. Leonard, M.D., Minneapolis,
Secretary of the Section of Materia Medica and
General Therapeutics.

Professor of Materia Medica and Therapeutics,
Homœopathic Medical Dept. of the University of Minnesota.

Dr. THOS. SKINNER, (*Corresponding Member, London.*)—Let every candidate read and carefully study every sentence of the first volume of Hahnemann's *Chronic Diseases* and his *Introduction* to each medicine recorded in the *Chronic Diseases* and *Materia Medica Pura;* and if he has time and inclination let him not fail to peruse the pathogeneses of Hahnemann recorded in these two remarkable works. Lastly, let him do his best to comprehend the spirit and the letter of the *Organon,* without a knowledge of which and a thorough belief in, no man can possibly practice the Homœopathy of Hahnemann.

Dr. E. T. BLAKE, (*Corresponding Member, London.*)—Though it may in some cases produce a stereotyped, inflexible physician, I would certainly not introduce Materia Medica nor Therapeutics till near the close of the curriculum. I take it that we are all agreed that students are taught too much, and that they remember too little.

Dr. J. W. HAYWARD, (*Corresponding Member, Birkenhead, Eng.*)—I would advise the student to spend most of his time and energies upon the *Cyclopædia of Drug Pathogenesy,* aided by Hughes', Dunham's and Farrington's and perhaps Hempel's *Lectures;* especially in passing the pathogenetic material through the "comparison" filter of Drs. Wesselhoeft and Sutherland, or (and?) that of the Baltimore Club, and in the preparation of at least one of the drugs for the Materia Medica, Physiological and Applied.

Prof. MOHR, (*Hahnemann of Phila.*)—Should embrace a general description of the non-metallic, vegetable and animal drug substances in their commercial or crude forms, and of the acids and special chemical products. The student should learn the methods required to convert these substances into the most active and least injurious medicinal forms, how these are administered, and what the maximum and minimum doses are. By carefully examining and handling specimens again and again he will become familiar with their characteristics.

JABEZ P. DAKE, M.D., Nashville,

Pioneer Professor of Materia Medica: Lectured on
Homœopathic Materia Medica in Philadelphia in 1855–6 and 7.

Prof. HINSDALE, (*Cleveland Univ. Med. and Surgery.*)—Dunham says it requires seven years persistent study to measurably master our Materia Medica. I think he is right: the pursuit of this most important subject in point of time is co-extensive with a student's and physician's professional studies.

Prof. McELWEE.—In the Homœpathic Medical College of Missouri it is customary to advise beginners to attend lectures, closely study the leading characteristics of the cardinal remedies, and endeavor to obtain only their "red-strings."

Prof. GILMAN, (*Hahnemann of Chicago.*)—First learn something of the rough work of the Materia Medica; the pharmacy and toxicological actions of the principal active poisons.

Prof. SNOW, (*Pulte of Cincinnati.*)—Do not attempt too much in Materia Medica; select a few drugs; for instance the polychrests, and thoroughly master them. Each drug should be studied by itself and not left until it has become a part of the student. Advises particular attention to the physiological and pathological provings.

Prof. J. HEBER SMITH (*Boston Univ. School of Med.*)—Cause the student to become fairly proficient in human anatomy, physiology, biology and elementary microscopy, general and medical chemistry; elementary botany; the history of medicine leading up to Homœopathy; also pharmaceutics, Latin formulæ and the *Organon.*

Prof. WESSELHŒFT, (*same school as above.*)—Devote much time to physics, (Natural Philosophy) chemistry, medical botany, and the brushing up of neglected Latin.

Prof. MACK, (*Ann Arbor.*)—Teach all the principles of medicine. When the field is once clearly mapped out, the student of Materia Med-

TIMOTHY FIELD ALLEN, A.M., M.D., LL.D., New York,

Professor of Materia Medica and Therapeutics,
New York Homœopathic Medical College and Hospital,
New York.

ica and Therapeutics is prepared to intelligently accept all that is good in any system of medicine. I would show the student just what empiricism is; what rational practice is; and the same as to Homœopathic practice. If the student happens to be acquainted with the philosophy of Swedenborg and came as a private pupil, he would be given a direct and positive argument in favor of Homœopathy. Scrupulously avoid all dogmatism. Only in the fields of pathology and drug pathogenesy can a question of Homœopathicity be determined. Use the following books: Taylor's *Treatise on Poisons*; the volume on poisons in Wharton and Stille's *Medical Jurisprudence;* Reese's *Medical Jurisprudence and Toxicology:* also a number of old school authorities on Materia Medica. Then follow with *Materia Medica Pura* schematically arranged; so that if a question arises, whether it be pathogenesy or not, the most critical investigation of the question in the field of science (*i. e.* pathogenesy and never therapeutics) will always be in order.

Prof. COWPERTHWAITE, (*Chicago Homœopathic.*)—Let them perfect themselves in botany and the chemistry of drugs, and follow with a study of the characteristic symptoms according to the Dr. Hering card plan. It is not wise to have students studying Materia Medica outside of these recommendations before they have listened to any lectures on the subject.

Prof. WOODWARD, (*Chicago Homœopathic.*)—They should obtain as distinct an idea of the toxical effects of drugs as they may from reading and comparing cases of poisoning. Also read Hughes' *Pharmacodynamics*, Taylor on *Poisons*, Wood's or Bartholow's *Materia Medica*, and *U. S. Dispensatory.*

Prof. ROYAL, (*Iowa University.*)— Give student Hughes' *Pharmacodynamics*, Dunham's *Lectures* and Farrington's *Clinical Materia Medica*. Look up all unfamiliar words and technical terms. Above all, do not let the student become disgusted with dry symptomatology.

R. E. DUDGEON, M.D., London.

Prof. DEWEY, (*Hahnemann of SanFrancisco*.)—Advises students to ground themselves well in the history of Homœopathy. Read Sharpe's *Tracts*, Dudgeon's *Lectures*, Ameke's *History*, and *Fifty Reasons for being a Homœopath*. ·

Prof. LEONARD, (*Univ. of Minn*.)—If he has not had preliminary college training, should learn something of botany, pharmacy and toxicology. If previously trained, should choose leading drugs in larger works on Toxicology, and Hughes' *Pharmacodynamics*. Also and better the *Cyclopædia of Drug Pathogenesy*.

Prof. EDGERTON, (*Kansas City College*.)—Select a work which gives general action of remedies and study them in groups and families, noting and memorizing the peculiar and characteristic symptoms.

Prof. PRICE, (*Baltimore—Southern Hom. Coll*.)—Pay no attention to details of symptomatology. Study botany and history of drugs. Occupy his attention with more preliminary studies.

Prof. CHEESEMAN, (*National of Chicago*.)—Study Hawkes' and Guernsey's *Key-notes*. Select from thirty to fifty polychrests, and endeavor to give him a good idea of these drugs.

Prof. NIELSEN, (*Late of National of Chicago*)—Acquire the physiological action of the principal drugs from Hughes' *Pharmacodynamics*, Shoemaker's or Bartholow' *Materia Medica*, Taylor on *Poisons*. Pay no attention to provings made from high potencies, but only such as have resulted from taking a tangible and reasonable dose.

Prof. HAWKES, (*Hering College*.)—Study the *Organon*. Read Farrington's *Materia Medica*, and Dunham's *Homœopathy: The Science of Therapeutics*. Give him an occasional case to look up. Also read carefully the *Homœopathic Pharmacopœia* and the *Life of Hahnemann*.

T. C. DUNCAN, M.D., Chicago,

President of the National Homœopathic Medical College
of Chicago.

Prof. H. C. ALLEN, (*Hering of Chicago.*)—Don't let him study Materia Medica until he attends lectures.

Prof. MONROE, (*Southwestern of Louisville.*)—Don't study Materia Medica in preparatory year. Ground the student in anatomy, physiology, chemistry, botany and pathology. Materia Medica is the pinnacle of the medical temple, the science toward which all other medical knowledge should ultimately converge.

Dr. GRAMM, (*Ardmore, Pa.*)—Familiarize the student with the nomenclature of his profession. Study the elementary steps of medicine. Be well grounded in botany, physiology and anatomy.

Dr. PECK, (*Providence.*)—Study Hughes' *Pharmacodynamics* at the very beginning.

Dr. KRAFT, (*Cleveland.*)—Give him Dunham's books to read; *talk*, not *read* the *Organon* to him.

GEORGE B. PECK, M.D., Providence, R. I.

Question 2.

Which is the best method of teaching Materia Medica:

(a)   For the preceptor to his student;

(b)   For the teacher to his class;

(c)   Give an outline of your method of studying or teaching a drug in the class-room.

Answers.

DR. DUDGEON.--The best mode of acquiring a knowledge of the action of medicine on the human body, i. e. of Materia Medica, is to study their pathogenetic effects as shown by individual provings and poisonings in such a work as the *Cyclopædia of Drug Pathogenesy*, and compare them with the therapeutic effects as detailed in some work like Hughes' *Pharmacodynamics*.

DR. HUGHES.—A teacher of Materia Medica in a college dominated by the method of Hahnemann should first of all ground his students in the pathogenetic action of drugs; and for this purpose he should use original material. When from these the sick-making power of the drug has been demonstrated, its power to heal should be exhibited and the two classes of action correlated. Eliminate from the class-room those compilations of symptomatology in which clinical symptoms are mixed up with pathogenetic and pathological hypotheses with observed facts in undistinguished mass. These are simply fatal to the student. I urge the teaching in our colleges of pure drug-pathogenesy based on original material.

A. LEIGHT MONROE, M.D., Louisville,

Professor of Materia Medica and Clinical Lecturer on
Orificial Surgery, Southwestern Homœopathic
Medical College, Louisville.

DR. SKINNER.—The student must be taught to rely more upon himself than upon the teacher, and the lecturer should teach his class to observe and reason and act as from themselves; if there is one object to be avoided more than another, it is dogmatic teaching. Dogmatic teaching has wrecked many a splendid thoughtsman; and as it is founded in the innate love of power and vanity of human nature, the sooner it is crushed out ot our schools and universities the better. Both preceptor and professor should direct the pupil to be everlastingly studying the Materia Medica, or, more properly speaking, the pathogeneses of remedies for themselves, beginning always with the polychrests and advancing by degrees to those remedies which are acknowledged to be least in request in practice, leaving out many or all which have been imperfectly proven in the healthy or sick. Every remedy should be shown to the student in its crude state. Every college should possess a museum of all the best specimens of Materia Medica from the animal, vegetable and mineral kingdoms, and every substance should be described classically and all its physical, chemical, microscopical, physiological and toxicological properties and habitat given before touching upon the pathogeneses. If museums are impracticable, then substitute plates or paintings of botanical specimens: and the student should be encouraged to collect the plants for himself. Materia Medica and Therapeutics are best studied together. Each student should be given the symptoms of a bona fide case; or let him take the notes, and teach him by the aid of reliable repertories and Materia Medica to find the nearest homœopathic remedy. This should be the beginning and ending of all homœopathic teaching of Materia Medica and Therapeutics, and it should form a daily part of the system of teaching. Dr. Carroll Dunham's *resumé* of a medicine as found in his *Science of Therapeutics* is the best method for teaching a class.

DR. BLAKE.—I look upon all didactic lectures as an elaborate and dignified way of wasting the time of the teacher and of the taught. Small tutorial classes with constant questions, students invited constantly without dreading ridicule to express difficulties—the thing to be

HOWARD CRUTCHER, M. D., Chicago,
Professor of Surgical Anatomy and Principles of Surgery
in the Hering Medical College and Hospital,
Chicago.

like a "peripatetic class" more personal and human--is the better way
of teaching Materia Medica.

Dr. HAYWARD.—The preceptor should select in the *Cyclopædia of
Drug Pathogenesy*, first a medicine with a well defined sphere of action,
such as cantharis; have his pupil study it well, and then examine him on
it. Afterwards select another a little more extended in its sphere and
repeat the process; then a polychrest and so on. Apply the same process to the class, and afterwards call upon them to select a medicine
and work it up for the Materia Medica, Physiological and Applied.

Prof. MOHR.—Teaching in the class room I consider best. The following outline of a study of pulsatilla is the plan I usually follow:
Common names. Description botanically and geographically. Active
principle. Its preparation. Its history, general and homœopathic.
Pathogenetic action. Therapeutics: (a), Old School; (b), Homœopathic. Comparisons, analogues, antidotes, inimicals and concordants.
Under the history division is given the fact, for instance that little was
known of the great powers of pulsatilla until Hahnemann proved it
(1806), since which time it has been constantly employed in homœopathic practice. The first homœopathic prescription in Pennsylvania
was pulsatilla 30, given to a case of dysmenorrhœa by Dr. Henry Det-
wiler, July 24, 1828.

Prof. HINSDALE.--In teaching the important remedies I go over
them, first giving the prominent symptoms as they may be presented in
the anatomical parts of the body; then give the therapeutic application
to the diseased conditions in which they are likely to be indicated.
Often, in giving the symptomatology, I begin with that part of the body
upon which the drug has the most marked action.

Prof. MCELWEE.—A preceptor should suggest a drug to the student
for study with the instruction to glean only its central or characteristic actions; then quiz him on the subject, in order to verify his correct impressions and correct wrong ones. In class-room it is the cus-

J. HEBER SMITH, M.D., Boston,

Professor of Materia Medica in Boston University
School of Medicine, Boston.

tom to inform the class of the subject of the next lecture; then, after having acquired thorough familiarity with the subject, present to them a drug (word) picture, accurately and artistically drawn, arranging and grouping the characters in such striking fashion that they will remain fixed firmly on the students' mind's eye, so that at the bed-side he will recognize its similar as soon as revealed. I think didactic lectures are the best, because it details the action of an individual drug, compares it with others in a given particular, and can be supplemented by quizzes subsequently.

Prof. GILMAN.—Day by day and hour by hour the preceptor should drop isolated hints and key-notes and therapeutic facts, collated from his own experience; to the student these will soon form anchorage ground for subsequent larger instruction. Give oral-didactic illustrations with typical cases. Compare with the same disorder pathologically as found under other remedies. Follow with frequent quizzes to enforce the lesson and clear up doubts. Give the history, habitat and character of the drug; make it short; always give the preparation. Then follow with poisonings, if there be any; from these violent effects select the characteristics. Compare these with the provings. Describe the tissues upon which it acts and the form of action. In this way the key-notes or characteristics of the drug are made far more intelligible to a student or a class.

Prof. MCMICHAEL.—A student connecting a few symptoms of a patient with those of a drug and noting the effect will have an object of interest and thereby receive an impression of the drug which he might commit to memory. In class I would advise the didactic method, giving briefly the physiological effect of the drug, the symptomatological characteristics only being alluded to; and then comparing these characteristics when possible with symptoms of other drugs which are identical in phraseology or symptoms, or which are similar in meaning, to the extent of four or five comparisons; at the same time bringing out some one or two peculiarities of each drug which will characterize it from the others. As for example:

W. A. DEWEY, M.D., New York,

Late Professor of Materia Medica and Therapeutics in the
Hahnemann Hospital College of San Francisco.

DRUGS.	PAIN IN LEFT OVARY.	DISTINCTION.
Cimicifuga.	Neuralgic pain in left ovary, extending up and down left side, also across the abdomen. Great tenderness on touch.	Direction of pain. Tenderness.
Graphites.	Swelling of left ovary with violent pain on touch and inspiration. Menses scanty and pale.	Swelling, Aggravation and Amelioration
Lachesis.	Violent pain in left ovary and sensitiveness to weight of clothes; relieved by menstrual flow. Hot flashes. Pains extend from left to right.	Sensitiveness Amelioration
Zincum.	Boring pain in left ovary, relieved by pressure and during menses. Fidgety feet.	Character of pain and Amelioration

Or the following:

DRUGS.	SENSATION OF A STONE IN STOMACH.	DISTINCTION.
Nux vom.	Sensation of a stone or weight in stomach. Tongue white, taste sour or bitter, worse an hour or so after eating. Scraped sensation in pit. Ugly at all times.	Disposition and Aggravation.
Bryonia.	Sensation in stomach as if a stone lay there. Sour taste. White tongue. Ugly when disturbed. Thirst.	Disposition and thirst.
Ars. alb.	Weight in stomach after eating as from a stone. Burning, tongue brown, dry red tip, thirst, anxiety. Restless.	Burning and Restlessness
Arg. nit.	Severe cardialgia as from a stone in stomach. Craving for sweets. Breath fetid, tongue white, red tip.	Craving and Breath.

CHAS. S. MACK, M.D., Ann Arbor,

Professor of Materia Medica and Therapeutics in
Homœopathic Medical Department of the
University of Michigan,
Ann Arbor.

In the first table the student gets a definite idea of a characteristic peculiar to four drugs, which is location; in the second he gets a symptom characteristic of four drugs, which is a sensation in the stomach. At the same time some peculiarity of each drug is given which differentiates it from the others. Studying the symptomatology in this manner the student will have at his command a knowledge of comparative Materia Medica which he can utilize to good advantage before the patient, always making (at least) an intelligent prescription.

Prof. SNOW.—The preceptor should teach Materia Medica to his student by giving particular attention to the physiological and pathological provings. Each drug should be studied by itself and should not be left until the student feels that it has become a part of himself. In a limited manner, then, symptomatology may be taken up. The preceptor should not be content with merely outlining the course of study, but should give both time and attention, hearing them recite and correcting false impressions and animating their minds with new zeal for the laborious study of Materia Medica. Teach him clinically as early and as much as possible, for a clinical fact will drive home and rivet the truth.

In the class-room clinical teaching cannot, in the nature of things, take first place; here it must be didactic with frequent questioning. Clinical material should be used. A graded course is just as desirable in Materia Medica as in other branches of medicine. Each drug may be taken up separately and its action upon the human system studied without reference to that of any other drug, or it may be compared with other drugs. In the first year the student should learn drug-action without reference to other drugs, spending most of his time in acquiring the physiological action and key-notes of twenty-five or thirty drugs. The second year the same, only enlarged; the third year the work should be largely comparative. By thus beginning and continuing the study in an orderly manner the student at his graduation will be better equipped than many practitioners of several years' standing educated according to the methods now in vogue in many colleges.

A. W. WOODWARD, M.D., Chicago,

Professor of Materia Medica and Therapeutics in the
Chicago Homœopathic Medical College,
Chicago.

I teach the drug by giving its name, both scientific and common; its kingdom, family species, habitat, and, if possible, a specimen of it is handed around for personal examination. Then I take up its preparation; one or two cases of poisoning are related, if there be any. The physiological action, its practical applications to disease, and the old and the homœopathic ways of usage. The next hour the lecture is gone over again, but in a greatly condensed form. When a sufficient number of remedies have been gone over in this way, then comparisons are instituted and quizzes. These comparisons and quizzes are directed to the end of bringing out all the information that can be gathered concerning the drug in question, peculiarities of climate, etc. It is certainly not an accident that the cinchona tree grows in an intensely malarial zone, while aconite is a native of mountainous regions where acute chills and congestions are frequent. It is quite rational to suppose that there is some relation between the diseases of a zone or region and the medicinal plants which flourish there. These general comparisons are followed by that dealing with their physiological action, namely, the organs and tissues which they affect and their mode of action.

Prof. J. HEBER SMITH.—I have found it advisable to direct the student's daily reading in fields rich with clinical material. Individual cases are better than any other means and serve to fix therapeutic knowledge. I place in his hands annual and monthly reports of medical societies. He is also encouraged to glean in other fields, it being thought that no harm can come from broad and liberal culture and familiarity with the current opinions and practice of all medical schools. In the class-room I give Latin name and English synonym; habitat, derivation, pharmaceutical preparations, general properties, action upon organic tissues both of animals and men; common medical uses of all times, with a sketch of its proving. Then minutely I sketch the characteristic symptoms, illustrating its action as a simile by occasional cullings from my clinical note-books. I adhere to the rubrics of Hahnemann, beginning with the mental symptoms. The drug's pathogenesy having now been given, there follows a statement of its relation-

W. B. HINSDALE, M.D., Cleveland,

Professor of Philosophical and Applied Materia Medica,
the Organon, and Clinical Medicine, in the
Cleveland University of Medicine and Surgery,
Cleveland.

ships. Lastly I give its administration, stating the usually approved dose and its repetition.

Prof. WESSELHOEFT.—Student and class are treated similarly. Requires that the student shall have a good college education, or at least its equivalent in languages, mathematics and general culture. Then the students are directed how to make short provings on themselves, several working together preferable; these provings are then to be compared with reliable collections as found, say, in Hughes' *Cyclopædia*. The students should also be instructed in Analysis of Provings; that is, a comparison of several provings of the same drug by different provers. I strenuously require that provings be judged as to their value by agreement of results obtained. This analysis being completed and written out in brief narrative form, they are next taught to make a repertorial arrangement of their narratives. Following this would come the clinical work. Pharmaceutical knowledge being involved in this work, attention to it is paid whenever required. In the class-room the work is necessarily didactic. An assistant divides the seniors into groups, giving each group a drug to prove. The didactic part, furthermore, includes the description and classification of medicinal substances; its origin and place in nature are first mentioned, its toxic effects explained and a comprehensive synopsis of its best provings given in narrative form. This history and results are related so that the students are constantly reminded that the provings represent a group of symptoms analogous to groups found in natural disease. I describe the pathogeneses of a drug precisely as I would the indications for a remedy. I ask them to imagine a case of illness characterized by certain symptoms; the student is then told such is the effect of arsenic belladonna, sulphonal, etc. In this way they habituate their minds to symptomatological work in comparison, comparing at once drug-effect and symptoms of natural disease. Neglect of pathological thinking is obviated; he is taught that a symptom of value as an indication is always of pathological value and should be distinguished from the manifold mere sensations which fill our text-books.

CHAS. MOHR, M.D., Philadelphia,

Professor of Materia Medica and Therapeutics in
Hahnemann Medical College and Hospital,
Philadelphia.

Prof. MACK.--Both individual student and class-room students should be first well prepared in the principles of medicine. Some preceptors have barely time sufficient to direct the student in his daily reading; but the teacher in the class-room may be expected to devote time necessary for personal inquiry into constantly arising questions. I counsel the avoidance of dogmatizing upon questionable points. Discuss the questions with the students, stating the *pros* and *cons* bearing upon each particular point and lead the student to correct conclusions; but let him also know that there are always questions that must remain unanswered. Don't for an instant let the student suppose that you or anyone else knows all of, for instance, *Materia Medica Pura*, or that your opinion, or that printed in a text-book, is necessarily final. Hunt down items recorded as pathogenesy to the original sources and encourage your students to do the same. I first give what seems of interest regarding the origin and history of the drug, its botany and chemistry. If a serious poison I state its effects, showing what are due to its dynamic properties and what to its physical or chemical properties. I take up old school writers and follow out the pathogenesy if the drug is one of which they treat. I point out that what is recorded by the old school under physiological action is not pathogenesy. For each drug that I teach I have made out a chart based upon toxicologies and old school Materia Medica and upon the *Cyclopædia of Drug Pathogenesy*. Of these charts I have made enough copies to put a chart of each drug into the hands of each student. Clinical symptoms and "clinical verifications" I do not put into the charts. I think that one who teaches them should always keep them distinct from records of pathogenesy. I give instruction regarding such rational practices and such empirical practices as commend themselves to me. I sometimes discuss some given practice advocated as rational by others, and point out what seems to me fallacious in it. No drug can be a homœopathic medicine unless it is a dynamic poison; therefore I do not lecture upon natrum mur. and carbo vegetabilis. Regarding Lycopodium I may say to the class: "I hardly think this is pathogenetic, and if not pathogenetic it cannot be homœopathic; but many homœopathists have regarded it as

HENRY SNOW, M.D., Cincinnati,

Professor of Materia Medica and Therapeutics in
Pulte Medical College, Cincinnati.

having such and such a pathogenesy and as curative when given upon such and such indications." I encourage students to ask questions regarding pathogenesy, and to discuss them with me in the lecture room, so that for a part of the lecture hour our exercises often become quite conversational.

Prof. COWPERTHWAITE.—The preceptor should give his student encouragement in the study of characteristic symptoms, and with these he must necessarily combine therapeutics. The teacher should interest his class, and this he cannot do by spending hour after hour in reading over a voluminous array of dry and uninteresting symptoms. Theoretically, the study of Materia Medica should be begun by acquiring a knowledge of symptomatology before attempting to make a general analysis of the action of a drug, or any practical application of it to disease; but practically we must admit that to the student who comes for the first time to the study of this important subject it is a very uninteresting task, only made the more so by being obliged to sit by the hour and listen to the teacher reading symptom after symptom with but an occasional comment upon the same. I give first the name and synonyms of the drug; then follow rapidly with a general outline of the action of the drug from the physio-pathological standpoint. I then take up the uses in disease, mentioning first the diseases in which it is most prominently useful, and in this connection I work in the symptomatology of the drug together with a comparison of other drugs. This excites the attention and interest of the student, for he sees at once that in acquiring a knowledge of that symptom he has a definite object in view. Generally, at the close of the lecture, I give a rapid *resume'* of the therapeutic uses of the drug and close by slowly reading from fifteen to twenty of its most important characteristic symptoms. These are written by the student on cards. I do not believe in giving the student too many symptoms; a few symptoms well learned are really worth more to the student than would be a mechanical memorization of the whole symptomatology of the Materia Medica.

THEO. NIELSEN, M.D., Chicago,

Late Professor of Materia Medica and Therapeutics in the
National Homœopathic Medical College
of Chicago.

Prof. WOODWARD.— I think both preceptor and teacher should seek to impress upon the student the importance of observing the order of development of drug action and the group of symptoms which characterize that remedy. This should be illustrated by cases already published, these being analyzed with a view both to the order of development and the symptoms which appear together. Then the sequence should be applied in the clinic, finding a remedy for the case according to the clinical history and concomitants of the affection.

Prof. ROYAL.—After my student has attended one or more courses of lectures I have him, when possible, listen while I take a case. After the patient is dismissed I have him give me the remedy and the reason for giving it. I then tell him what I give and the reason. When making my visits I carry a note-book and jot down the symptoms. On my return to the office I tear out the leaves, give them to my student for a repetition of the process mentioned above. In the class-room I give a brief outline of the physiological or toxicological effect of the drug. I then fill in the characteristic symptomatology of the various regions of the body, usually the black type and italics of Allen's *Hand-Book*. I then give clinical application and compare the different remedies most frequently used for a certain disease. In the quiz I pay special attention to this comparison. I ask one student to give me the symptoms in intermittent fever for which he would prescribe capsicum; another one the symptoms for bryonia; then another student is required to give the points of difference between the two.

Prof. DEWEY.—A good way would be for the student to prepare himself upon a certain drug and then be thoroughly quizzed. In the class-room I endeavor to grade my teaching. First year students are required to memorize a certain number of characteristics, not exceeding ten of each drug lectured upon. Some drugs will have but one which I insist upon their learning. One year I give all the drugs of the vegetable kingdom; the second year the animal and mineral kingdoms, as well as nosodes. I teach Materia Medica and Therapeutics together, giving

L. C. McElwee, M.D., St. Louis,

Co-Professor of Materia Medica and Therapeutics, and of
Drug Pathogenesy, in the Homœopathic Medical
College of Missouri, St. Louis.

first the origin of the drug and its mode of preparation--its physiological action and its characteristic homœopathic action. In most drugs I follow the Hahnemannian scheme, commencing with the mental symptoms. I do not give a large number of comparisons, because they tend to confuse the student. I rely largely upon my quizzes. In the quiz I do not confine myself to one drug; the student never knows upon what subject he will be quizzed. A favorite way of mine is to give a quiz one day upon, for instance, the constipation of different remedies, comparing one with the other. Another day upon the application of different drugs to chest affections; another day upon the action of the eye. If I find the class deficient upon any one heading I usually stick to that heading until it becomes familiar.

Prof. LEONARD.—Preceptor should select typical drugs—those most commonly indicated—and when these are mastered he should illustrate their action by clinical cases, finally permitting the student himself to prescribe. In the class-room no clinical work should be undertaken until the beginning of the third year I teach the nomenclature, emphasizing popular names, natural history or chemistry, pharmacy, old school and new, drug history especially, as it bears upon homœopathy, toxicology, by brief but typical cases, both of chronic and of acute poisonings; physiological action which should include a short explanation of its supposed effects upon the tissues; old school *resume'* of therapeutics, homœopathic therapeutics, not necessarily in anatomical order; relationships, comparisons and the dosage.

Prof. EDGERTON.—The preceptor should place into the student's hands Hull's *Jahr's Symptomatology*, or Farrington's *Clinical Materia Medica*. Let him then begin with aconite, leaving out comparisons; after reading it a few times, question the student to see what he has remembered, pointing out carefully its sphere of action and emphasizing its more characteristic action. Then take up another member of the same family and proceed as before; then compare the two remedies, noting their points of similarity and dissimilarity; follow this with quiz

JAMES E. GILMAN, M.D., Chicago,

Professor of Materia Medica and Therapeutics, and
Institutes of Medicine,
Hahnemann Medical College and Hospital of Chicago.

on imaginary case, to draw out which one of the remedies is indicated. In the class-room I use the comparative method. I name the remedy, give its natural order, also mentioning other prominent members of the same class; give its habitat, botanical history, its general history and early uses. Then I speak of its active principle, its smallest fatal dose, if poisonous, and cite cases of poisoning, dwelling especially on the symptoms occurring prior to death. Then give post-mortem appearance and antidotal treatment. The provings are next taken up and the effects of non-fatal doses are described and dilated upon. Pathological detail is then entered into with differential diagnosis, occasionally bringing in cases from actual practice. I seek to keep the student interested, referring as little to notes or manuscript as possible. Next day I quiz rigidly and give a synopsis of the lecture we have gone over.

Prof. PRICE.--I do not know that there is a best method of private instruction. That student will best understand the homœopathic application of drugs who is best informed as to all the various effects produced by drugs and the various uses to which they have been and still are put by the various schools of medicine. Preceptors should teach just such things to their students, but at the same time point out the advantages of the scientific or homœopathic method of using drugs compared with the cruder, unscientific methods of the ol er school. The general effects of drugs upon the healthy should be taught with an occasional detail of prominence which is characteristic of the given drug.

In the class-room I teach the difference between the several therapeutic methods, i. e., antipathy, allopathy, isopathy, homœopathy, etc., showing what each means, and by thus contrasting the methods and their several spheres of usefulness endeavor to beget at the very start a confidence in the law of similars. In this preliminary study I give the various classifications of drugs according to the old school idea; astringents tonics, stimulants, sedatives, etc., ending with alteratives, which latter I use as a bridge between heterodox medicine and Homœopathy, calling attention to the fact that alterative medicine is but Homœopathy

W. O. CHEESEMAN, M.D., Chicago,

Professor of Materia Medica and Clinical Therapeutics
in the National Homœopathic Medical
College of Chicago.

under a different name. I further teach that the modern "physiological medicine" is also a crude sort of Homœopathy. I endeavor to instill the idea that there is but one way to find out what are the real pathogenetic effects of a drug, and that this way is through experimentation upon the healthy human being. I teach that a preliminary health record is one of the absolute necessities to a scientific proving; that with it a homœopathic physician can fulfill the previsional possibilities of Homœopathy and with certainty prescribe the proper drug for the given condition without having had previous clinical experience with the drug. This may seem like dangerous doctrine for minds not fully tutored, because there are so few really scientific drug experiments. If it be dangerous to teach truth, then this is a dangerous doctrine; the fact remains that however scientific may be the theory of Homœopathy, the practical working system upon which the practitioner depends is approximately scientific only. The Materia Medica needs strengthening in the department of pathogenesy. The class-room is the place to sow this seed. In taking up a remedy for lecture I review the history of the drug, its general sphere of action, its detailed symptomatology, its relation to disease; and, finally, its analogues are discussed. I endeavor to familiarize the student with the practical details of the drug's action in conjunction with that of its analogues, so that when he finds indications for the given drug at the bed-side he will also have presented to his mind a picture of the group of synergists from which he may select the drug best suited to the case.

Prof. CHEESEMAN.—I would select about thirty to fifty of the leading remedies, mostly polychrests, and endeavor to give the student and class a good idea of these drugs, both by didactic and clinical instruction. I believe that it is better for our students to go out from our colleges with a thorough knowledge of from thirty to fifty drugs than to give them a smattering of two hundred.

Prof. HAWKES.--The preceptor should select many remedies having many symptoms in common and a few in each characteristic, and urge

S. F. SHANNON, M.D., Denver.

the student to study these carefully, so as to be able to answer the preceptor when asked for similar symptoms, and also for dissimilar or
characteristic symptoms; he should be given typical cases to study up
from the Materia Medica. In the class-room my plan is to give a general outline of the sphere of action of each remedy, then its characteristic symptoms. The latter I urge to commit to memory. I then compare remedies having a similar sphere of action, noting the characteristic symptoms distinguishing each from all others. In quizzing the
classes on the preceding lectures I sometimes give a characteristic symptom and ask the student to name the remedy. In other instances I will
state a case and ask which remedy corresponds to the symptoms of this
case. Then again I name a few symptoms of a remedy and ask the student to state how he will ascertain whether that remedy is the right
one; in other words, I partially make up the case and ask him to complete it.

Prof. ALLEN, H. C.--I teach what is characteristic of each drug—its
modalities, its complement, its acute or chronic symptoms, what remedies precede or follow best, comparisons with other remedies, etc., and
how it differs from others to which it is naturally allied.

Prof. MONROE.--The preceptor should take his student with him as
much as possible and cite prescriptions, when opportunity offers, of
interesting and typical cases. Also by appealing to his eyes with dia-
grams and perhaps to his ears with acrostics; by giving the general
action, the genius of the drug under consideration in a concise way; by
making an individual of the drug and comparing it carefully with drugs
that are related to it either by family ties, clinically or pathologically.
In the class-room I generally begin the year by teaching the classes that
drugs should be studied pathologically, symptomatologically and com-
paratively; that they are related by family ties; are inimical or un-
friendly; are complementary or friendly; are analogous; are antidotal
and concordant. I then give them twelve so-called "aphorisms," which
are general principles though not always applicable, but giving food

THOS. SKINNER, M.D., London.

tor much thought: One of these is: "Acid conditions are those of debility and generally associated with an irregular pulse. All the acids in
the Materia Medica have in their symptomatology debility with irregular
pulse." Another: "Where there is rapid tissue combustion there is
generally anxiety and thirst, as under aconite and arsenic." I only attempt to treat the polychrests thoroughly, and fix the smaller drugs in
the mind by comparison with some polychrest. My aim throughout is
to make my students think and philosophize, and to discourage the
parrot-like memorizing of symptoms, for the existence of which they
can give no reason. Some of my work is like scaffolding thrown
around a house while being built, which is easily thrown aside when the
work is complete.

Dr. GRAMM--The preceptor should give his student, in an explanatory
manner, the most important (pathogenetic) part of the general range of
each drug, beginning with the polychrests and add two or three characteristic symptoms that have been abundantly verified. He should also
take the student into his office with the most of his patients to teach
him Materia Medica and practice in actual cases. In the class-room he
should divide the drugs for consideration, starting with the polychrests,
into groups or families to which they belong according to their similarity, beginning with their joint actions and give two or three characteristics, pathogenetic or clinical, showing the family relation as well as
their dissimilarity. Second year act upon the same principle, but widen
scope. Third and fourth year teach Materia Medica in its whole extent,
following the usual form of beginning with the name and history and
going through with the use and abuse, preparation, generalities, all
symptoms, etc.

Dr. NIELSEN.--I describe the drug in question, taking up its physiological action. Here I lay great stress, believing that symptomatology
and the finer details are uninteresting and easily forgotten; further, mere
symptomatology is often misleading if a good understanding of the
drug's physiological action has not been previously mastered. I do not

Conrad Wesselhœft, M.D., Boston,

Professor of Pathology and Therapeutics in
Boston University School of Medicine,
Boston.

exclude symptomatology; on the contrary I would encourage the students, especially during the last year, to study symptomatology thoroughly, but not in the same manner as a child studies his a, b, c. The desire of mankind is to know the whys and wherefores, and this is true also of medicine.

Dr. PECK.--When a student has possessed himself of the *Pharmacodynamics* his instructor should take him into each available sick-chamber, and upon retiring inform him of the prescription and the reasons why; also what other remedies suggested themselves. The physiologial properties of the remedy in question would thus prominently be brought out as well as the characteristic symptoms. The youth will then read up the subject in detail at his leisure. The instructor will naturally question him on the matter as they pay subsequent visits. The teacher should use lectures. These should be dogmatic (the office confers authority); he should be concise and correct to date. The lecturer should describe the effect of the ingestion of a large quantity of the substance under discussion, carefully discriminating between the phenomena resulting merely from its physical nature and those produced by the penetration of more or less of its particles into the organism. This brings him to its so-called physiological properties. He is now prepared to present a rational explanation of the bulk of its symptomatology, and, without discredit, frankly to admit that the indication of the organic relationship of other established specified characteristics must await additional advances in allied departments of science. He should emphasize always the difference between the physiological and the curative action of medicaments, that his pupils may everywhere be able to distinguish between cures and recoveries on the one hand and natural deaths and manslaughters on the other. He should fix in the pupil's mind that while observed phenomena are as fixed and definite as the established order of nature, their explanations are as evanescent as the tints of sunset, entertained only until others more satisfactory shall be devised.

GEORGE ROYAL, M.D., DesMoines,

Professor of Materia Medica and Therapeutics in the
Homœopathic Medical Department of the
State University of Iowa,
Iowa City.

Dr. KRAFT.—The preceptor should teach his student from Dunham's works and also keep him well supplied with talks from the *Organon*. For the class-room the professor should *talk* his remedies—never read them. He should use blackboard and chalk—chalk-talks. He should omit the unsubstantial and disputed or contradictory things and confine the talk, aided by a few general notes to guide the trend of the lecture, to the essentials of the remedy in question. He should so direct his remarks that the characteristic points of the remedy will be repeatedly and repeatedly forced to the notice of the student or class and dwelt upon. He should discourage note-taking. Manuscript-reading in the professor is as painful a blunder as note-taking in the student. It is not what is taken down that is of value, but only what is remembered. Ask the class to give its whole attention to listening and understanding; explain that the historical and statistical parts of the remedy may be easily found in any text-book, and require them to read that up before the next lecture. Reason with the class, using physiology, anatomy, botany, pathology, therapeutics—in short, every resource of nature and art should be called into requisition to make the subject attractive, for what attracts, interests, and what interests, teaches. If any part of the lecture-talk seems ambiguous to the student, permit him, nay, encourage him, to interrupt the teacher and have it explained. Endeavor to put the remedy into a picture; individualize it, make it an entity, put it into clothes; give the student something to hold on to, something that he can remember as the totality. Avoid the teaching of bare symptomatology or the studying of isolated characteristics, however strong they may seem. Materia Medica should be taught in every year of the course. Every chair in a homœopathic college should have a surpassing regard for the Materia Medica chair, and give all possible aid instead of casting mild ridicule upon its efforts.

MARK EDGERTON, M.D. Kansas City,

Professor of Materia Medica and Therapeutics in the
Kansas City Homœopathic Medical College,
Kansas City, Mo.

Dr. SAMUEL A. JONES, (*Ann Arbor.*) — I never thought that I knew "the best method of teaching Materia Medica," though I certainly recognized great differences in the various methods that came under my observation.

I have never known a *preceptor* who taught any method; the student was simply turned loose into the mazes of our symptology like a calf in a pasture; if he found digestible material, well and good; if he didn't, *ditto*.

I have found students and practitioners to be divisible into two classes: the *mechanical* (overwhelmingly in the majority) and the *philosophical* (nearly as scarce as hens' teeth). The 'Materia Medica" of the first class is a crazy-quilt of "key-notes," "characteristics" and "guiding symptoms," and the owner thereof can do nothing for a "case" in which he does not find a symptom or symptoms corresponding to one or more of his patches. The limit of his symptom-list is (for him) the limit of the capabilities of that remedy. The Materia Medica of the second class is a comprehension and an apprehension of the *genius* of the several remedies that he has studied. He does not recognize Cromwell by his wart, or Wellington by his nose, but measures them by their campaigns; he knows the resources of their generalship and can fight his battles like them.

It seems to me that the method of their studying Materia Medica is two-fold. It begins with toxicology to get the broad outlines and the pathological consequences of the drug's action, and this indicates the territory or territories that the drug principally affects. The information thus gained is the lamp by which to read the pathogenesis obtained from provings *in corpore sano*. The ear must be trained to catch the fainter pathogenetic notes that are lost in the fury of the toxicological storm; and when these are gotten their nature is such that they are indeed to the Jews a stumbling block and to the Greeks foolishness.

From these two sources, poisonings and provings, the student learns to recognize the *genius* of the remedy. He discerns the manner and nature of its attack, the localities in which it is peculiarly puissant, its idiosyncracies (which its modalities really are), and the conditions under

ELDRIDGE C. PRICE, M.D., Baltimore,

Professor of Materia Medica and Therapeutics in the
Southern Homœopathic Medical College,
Baltimore, Md.

which its action is intensified or mitigated (aggravations and ameliorations).

So far this is what I have presumed to call the philosophical study of Materia Medica. It is only the apprenticeship that precedes the practical application thereof. At this stage many practitioners make the mistake of trying to find the Materia Medica in the disease instead of the disease in the Materia Medica. If the distinction is not intelligible the reader may rest assured that his is a case of "arrested development," and he is in that embryonic condition wherein one laughs at him who uses Boenninghausen's "Therapeutic Pocket-Book." Nevertheless he may rest assured that until he becomes a faithful disciple of that master of therapeutics he will not realize the resources of the homœopathic Materia Medica.

Then the philosophical student of Materia Medica will supplement the toxicological and the pathogenetic investigation of a remedy with the comparative study of it by means of Boenninghausen's treatise. And such study is the most fruitful when it is made in an actual case. It brings out the relative values of symptoms and teaches on which to lay the stress even when a remedy is studied by itself; but with a case in hand it is the only method by which one can escape becoming a routinist instead of a therapeutist. To practice without it is to endeavor to find the Materia Medica in the disease instead of the disease in the Materia Medica.

[The address on *Natrum muriaticum* is submitted as an example of the initial study of that remedy after the method herein suggested.]

Dr. BOJANUS, (*Samara, Russia.*)—It is equally important for the student to visit the allopathic clinics at the same time as homœopathic to notice the difference in the indications and to study the results. The clinical teaching of Materia Medica must be carried on so that the teacher, after having examined in detail a certain case, both objectively and subjectively, should make his pupils choose the remedy themselves and give the reasons of their choice. Several pupils thus questioned would probably point at different remedies, but as only one can be the

A. C. COWPERTHWAITE, M.D., Chicago,

Professor of Materia Medica and Therapeutics in
Chicago Homœopathic Medical
College, Chicago.

right one the professor has to make the differential diagnosis of the different remedies and prove to the students for what reason one, several or all the remedies selected by them are not the right ones. I do not think that there is any method more suitable and more conducive to study alone than the method of Farrington of reading lectures upon Materia Medica; and if for the present the teacher takes these as a model he will certainly commit no blunder.

A. ROGER MCMICHAEL, M.D., New York,

Professor of Materia Medica and Therapeutics in
New York Medical College and
Hospital for Women,
New York.

Question 3.

Which is the best place for teaching therapeutics: hospital, dispensary, clinic, class room or bedside? And how should it be done?

Answers.

Dr. DUDGEON.—The discovery of similarity between medicinal effects on the healthy and disease symptoms constitutes homœopathic therapeutics. The perfection of homœopathic therapeutics would be a pathological similarity between medicine and disease; in other words, a morbid change in functions, sensations and organic structure. In our present pathological knowledge we cannot always find this thorough resemblance, so we are forced to depend upon a semblance thereof—the symptoms objective and subjective. We must endeavor to find a medicine having the greatest number of similar symptoms to that found in the diseased condition. The treatment by what is called the "key-note" symptoms is to be deprecated as an *ignis fatuus*. Hahnemann's occasional approval of allopathic or palliative therapeutics is well instanced in his use of camphor, which he recommends in influenza as a "palliative, but an invaluable palliative." In these cases homœopathic therapeutics were abandoned temporarily. Camphor in large doses produced choleraic symptoms, but if given as homœopathists the dose

W. J. HAWKES, M.D., Chicago,

Professor of Materia Medica and Clinical Medicine in
Hering Medical College and Hospital,
Chicago.

would be small. A practical knowledge of therapeutics will be best acquired by diligently observing the treatment of a competent physician in hospital and dispensary practice, and in listening to lectures.

Dr. SKINNER —There is no best place for teaching a drug in the homœopathic therapeutics. Hospitals, dispensaries, clinics or bedsides, all are first-rate; but in the class room it can be only elementary and not practical. I learned all I do know by at first practising (on the sly) on my allopathic patients, studying each case as it turned up by the light of the Materia Medica and the aid of repertories to the same. And I know no better way, after having mastered the *Organon* and *Chronic Diseases* and *Materia Medica Pura*.

Dr. BLAKE.—The only two places to teach treatment are probably bedside for acute diseases, and dispensary for chronic diseases; but no man learns his remedies till he has his own patients. The only way, I think, to teach a drug is by comparison with its *congeners*, noting carefully resemblances and differentiæ.

Dr. HAYWARD.—The best way of teaching therapeutics is by clinical lectures to students who can and will watch the cases in hospital or at the bedside. Dispensary work is too routine; hospital work too surgical; and the class-room too theoretical.

Prof. MOHR.—Therapeutics should be taught in the class room, and impressed on the mind, at the bedside, hospital and in dispensary practice; ample opportunities being given to the student to prescribe for patients and to watch the effects of medication.

Prof. HINSDALE.—I would answer clinically as far as possible and in the class-room anyhow.

Prof. McELWEE.—The best place for teaching therapeutics is in the clinic, if the class is together; and for individuals, at the bedside. It

H. C. ALLEN, M.D., Chicago,

Professor of Materia Medica and the Organon in
Hering Medical College and Hospital,
Chicago.

should be done by instilling into the student's mind the importance and art of properly taking the case; by teaching him the inductive method, and then substituting the drug-image for the disease picture.

Prof. GILMAN.—Each and every one of these has its place—its especial advantages and uses; all are desirable, none can be omitted without decided loss.

Prof. MCMICHAEL.—At hospital, dispensary or clinic by first obtaining the pathological condition which often is a part of the patient's most important symptomatology, as well as the drug that closely resembles it.

Prof. SNOW—Bedside teaching of therapeutics has given excellent results. The student under careful supervision is allowed to handle the case himself, studying the symptoms and choosing the remedy, which choice is either confirmed or corrected by the physician in charge.

Prof. J. HEBER SMITH.—The present demands on medical practitioners seem to require all these advantages stated in the question for development and thoroughness. I have come to believe that a well-equipped fair-sized hospital is superior in advantages for the student to all others even though circumstances seem to render the rules as to the student's visits somewhat imperatively exclusive, at least for the greater number. It can usually be arranged to afford more or less completely hospital experiences of golden value to every student attending a metropolitan school of medicine.

Prof. WESSELHŒFT.—The student having been well drilled and quizzed concerning pathology and therapeutics, may yet turn to the bedside, where under competent guidance he may readily comprehend cases presented to him. I am in the habit of admitting only senior students to the attendance of clinical cases. I inform myself thoroughly of the nature of these cases, of which each student of a group has one

Edward T. Blake, M.D., London.

assigned to him for examination, diagnosis and treatment, which he is directed to write out. At other times it is proper for the instructor to examine patients in the presence of students, demonstrating all the methods of physical and oral examination. In this process it is particularly desirable that the teacher should dwell on the importance of apparently trivial symptoms which may lead to correct choice of remedies. The student should be taught to deal conscientiously with tiresome cases and never show himself to be wearied by ceaseless repetition.

Prof. MACK.—Both theoretical and practical teaching must be done. In each prescription purporting to be homœopathic let the indications for the remedy be very definitely stated; whenever a rational practice (as distinguished from homœopathic) is adopted, let the theory for the prescription be clearly stated. When a purely empirical prescription is made or an empirical consideration modifies the prescription, the fact should be brought out.

Prof. COWPERTHWAITE.—The best place for teaching therapeutics is "everywhere." I think class-room teaching should come first. It is very rarely that an opportunity is afforded to teach materia medica at the bedside except in hospital cases, and indeed I am of the opinion that there is more of the latter in the college announcements than in fact. The longer I have experience as a teacher the more I realize the necessity of extensive clinical work in order to make a thorough, broad-minded and successful physician. The student who is only taught his therapeutics in the lecture room may prove himself an exceedingly smart man theoretically, but will be unfitted for the duties of his profession. I believe that the law should require the teaching of therapeutics through the dispensary and the clinic in a thorough and systematic manner before any student receives a diploma.

Prof. WOODWARD.—I think that it is desirable that senior students should have charge of the patients in clinic under my supervision, both for diagnosis of disease and of the remedy.

Prof. SAMUEL A. JONES, M.D., Ann Arbor, Mich.
The author of "The Grounds of a Homœopath's Faith."

Prof. ROYAL.—The best place to teach therapeutics is that place which will bring the student and patient together. I always want my students to make a diagnosis in each case. I have them tell which symptom they counted the most prominent and why, and then for what group of symptoms they selected the remedy given.

Prof. DEWEY.—I believe the hospital the best place for teaching therapeutics, for there the patient can be kept under absolute control and observation; there is no chance for other influences than the remedial one being used, and the patient is kept under observation until death or discharge. Whereas, in dispensary, clinic or class-room we are apt to lose sight of the patient after the first prescription, and at the bedside there is the uncertainty of our instructions not being carefully adhered to.

Prof. LEONARD.—All five as opportunity affords. No place has any advantage over the other unless it be the bedside with a small class of students; but all should be preceded by the drill in drug action outlined in the class room, and when possible by actual experiments upon drugs by the individual members of the class under the teacher's supervision. Bedside teaching should consist of demonstration of the patient's objective and subjective conditions by the teacher; and, as the students become more experienced, the offering of both diagnosis and prescription by them instead of the teacher. This method when applied to the wards of a hospital or in private practice seems to me to greatly excel any clinic or dispensary work, where the interval between the prescriptions and the uncertainty of other elements in the therapeutics of the case lessen the students' opportunities for appreciating the action of the medicine.

Prof. EDGERTON.—The therapeutics of acute diseases can be best taught at the bedside. Chronic cases can be nicely handled at the clinic. If the class be large the only practical way is to run the beds from hospital into lecture room, allow a number of the class to question patient and note down answers under the direction of the professor in charge; then call upon different members of the class for remedy and reasons for the prescription; then let the professor prescribe and tell wherein the different prescriptions were at fault and the reason for his own remedy.

Prof. PRICE.—Therapeutics should be taught in all these ways—in the hospital, in the dispensary, in the general clinic, and in the class room. Allow the students to be present at the bedside in the hospital when the examination and prescription are made, and give permission to visit from time to time during the whole course of illness. Let him prescribe for a patient under the supervision of the physician in charge of the dispensary. In the general clinic let him give close attention to the lecturer, who should call the attention of the student to the pathology and symptomatology upon which the various prescriptions are based. The student should attend the lectures with regularity and pay close attention to the views expressed and the facts stated.

Prof. CHEESEMAN.—I believe the clinic is the best place for instruction in therapeutics.

Prof. HAWKES.—In my judgment the best place for teaching therapeutics is in the clinic. My plan is to examine the patient physically and orally in the presence and hearing of the class, repeating aloud and emphasizing the symptoms I regard as valuable. I then ask the class individually to prescribe. This each does by writing on a slip of paper prepared for the purpose the number of the case, the remedy prescribed and the prescriber's name. I offer a reward each year to the student who shall prove to have most often prescribed the right remedy during the term.

Prof. ALLEN, H. C.—Wherever a sick patient is to be found. It should be done as laid down in the *Organon*. Treat the patient, not the disease.

Prof. MONROE.—In class-room and bedside. During the student's life and early practice hospital and dispensary work is too rushing, and does not give the student proper time for the complex and to him difficult intellectual problem necessary for the making of a good homœopathic prescription.

Dr. GRAMM.—The best place is undoubtedly at the bedside, in the hospital, by demonstrating on the subject the disease present, examining the patient in the manner as laid down by Hahnemann in his *Organon*, then prescribing and giving the reasons for the prescription according to the symptoms of the case and to the peculiarities of the patient. But as to teaching therapeutics in dispensaries, clinics or class-rooms exclusively, time, convenience and results will decide against. Yet there is no want of occasions in special cases to teach therapeutics in dispensaries and clinics and in the class-room, which is the usual place for teaching therapeutics, perhaps, in all colleges; theoretical symptomatology and practical application are separated to a disadvantage, and the instructions lack the illustrations and verifications of the proper therapeutical measure employed when offered at the bedside in the hospital. Here it makes a lasting impression upon the mind of the student and qualifies him for a good family physician. The homœopathic physician must be a diagnostician to be very successful.

Dr. PECK.—All these are equally well adapted to the teaching of therapeutics, provided each student can see and hear all there is to be seen or heard. In the class-room alone can a complete and systematic knowledge of this science be imparted. After the pathology of the special case or subject has been sufficiently elucidated, the remedies most generally indicated should be mentioned with the grounds of their adaptation to the disease and its special types.

Dr. KRAFT.—Therapeutics for the student is best taught in the college dispensary—indeed the dispensary should be the school of therapeutics;

it is the most readily accessible opportunity for furnishing clinical and therapeutical material, unless a hospital be attached. But in the latter case usually the rules of the hospital forbid the visitings from students except on rare occasions. The professor of therapeutics should be a chair by itself; and he should have charge of the dispensary, making it the supply depot for the college. The records should be so kept that by looking them over he may select the appropriate material illustrating his day's work, and thus give a lesson in the examination of patients for dynamic wrongs; at the same time explain the action of the remedy recommended, what it is expected to accomplish, why this or that potency is recommended and how much of the remedy shall be given. Or the entire senior class should be taken into the dispensary and taught how to examine the applicants for medical aid. The dispensary should be kept as much if not more for the benefit of the college, who pays for it, as for the benefit of the public, who pay nothing. In the hospitals and maternities surgical and obstetrical cases are mainly treated, and much good can be had there for materia medica and therapeutical instruction; but the tendency in the student's mind in such cases is more towards the mechanical than the dynamic.

Dr. BOJANUS.—Therapeutics and pharmacology are one. It must be taught practically. Theoretic lectures upon homœopathic therapeutics are not to be thought of till one is in condition to read lectures. If homœopathic therapeutics cannot be taught for the present otherwise than practically, then the best place for learning is a clinical hospital.

Question 4.

Do you teach the potency of the remedy studied? If not; why not? If you do, how do you explain the potency you advocate?

Answers.

Dr. DUDGEON.—Potency is a secondary consideration. The chief thing is the adaptation of the remedy to the characteristic symptoms of the disease in accordance with the rule *similia similibus curentur*. If that is made out satisfactorily it matters little what "potency" is employed, provided that the medium is not given too strong or so weak as to be incapable of producing curative action. As it is a rule of art not to use complicated means where simple means will suffice, it would be an infringement of this rule to give an excessively diluted medicine when a less diluted preparation will effect the desired result. The so-called "high-potencies," of which there are many, are variously prepared, having only this in common that they are diluted with an impure menstruum and are of unknown and uncertain strength, should not be preferred to the Hahnemannian preparations, which are made with a pure diluting menstruum and are of uniform and known strength.

Dr. HUGHES.—I would advocate here the historical method. It is not, I think, individual dicta that the student should hear from the chair of materia medica, but the general experience of the homœopathic body. There are medicines in favor with all sections, high-potency and low-potency men alike; there are those—like Calcarea and Sepia—which the latter scarcely think of; and there are those—like the alkaloids — which seem unknown in the practice of the former. Let the lecturer state these facts and refer each medicine to its proper class.

Dr. SKINNER.—I believe in all potencies from the tincture to the M. M. (F. C.), if selected according as Hahnemann directs in his *Organon*; and I have the utmost confidence in the higher attenuations. My experience of them extends now over 18 years.

Dr. BLAKE.—The potency I teach is that we should give as little as possible to children and as much as you can to the aged.

Dr. HAYWARD.—I would teach the "doses," but would drop the word "potency" and use "attenuation". I explain the power of medicine by the "attenuation" or attenuating process, or effect, enabling the particles or atoms of the medicine to join in the metabolic action in the formation of the nucleoli, or the primary preparation of the matter for the formation of the nucleoli, of the cells of the protoplasm of the nerves and tissues. There is no medicinal power separate from medicinal substance; but wherever there is medicinal substance—however minute in quantity—there is medicinal power, and one single atom may pervert, or restore, normal action to one cell.

Prof. MOHR.—I teach that there is no law governing the potency. Dosage is a matter of susceptibility and each patient must receive a dose large enough to produce a remedial effect, and yet small enough to prevent drug aggravation.

Prof. HINSDALE.—Yes, usually teach it in the clinical department. I do not advocate any potency numerically. In the pharmacy I detail the various ways of potentizing and numbering the potencies; but, clinically, when I say high, I am understood to mean about the 200th; middle, about the thirteenth; and low about the second to the twelfth. I make no claim to party membership in either extremity of the potency. The features of the particular case enter into the selection of the power of the remedy.

Prof. McELWEE.—Yes. We explain that the least possible amount that will cure must be used; that a remedy in infinitesimal quantities will act many times when the crude material will not; or if the crude material will act on account of the sensitiveness of the patient to its action alarming symptoms or poisonous effects are liable to be easily incurred by the exhibition of such crude material.

Prof. GILMAN.—I speak of the potencies, frequently stating the ones I use or have found serviceable. At the same time the potency is largely a matter of experience and not a scientific essential. I recommend to each to determine for himself what potency to use.

Prof. McMICHAEL.—I do not teach potency. If I am asked what potency to give I always mention the one I prefer, with the explanation that so long as the dose does not produce an aggravation I am satisfied, but not having a law to guide us in the choice of potency, it becomes a matter of experience which varies with each individual.

Prof. SNOW.—As no law of potency has yet been discovered and a great difference of opinion exists in the profession concerning this point, I carefully refrain from teaching the potency. Especially since I believe that both high and low potencies are valuable, and that the superiority of one or the other is a matter of individual judgment. Therefore, I leave the student in perfect freedom to choose for himself: when quoting cases of cure, however, the potency used is always given when known.

Prof. MACK.—I do not teach potency. I advise students to go slow if they tend to accept a belief in high potencies.

Prof. COWPERTHWAITE.—I do not teach potency because I do not believe it is a legitimate part of a teacher's duty. It is a matter of individual experience, and I think it would be assuming a great deal if the teacher should insist upon his class following any idea he may have in regard to potency, when possibly he might be the only member of the faculty entertaining such ideas. When I give any potency at all I explain that it is simply my experience. I advise them to endeavor to use the higher potencies, simply to give them encouragement in this direction. The potency with very many students is very low, and for this reason I think it is wise to encourage them to use the higher potencies as they will drop to the low potencies soon enough any way in most cases, probably too soon, and too low rather than too high.

Prof. WOODWARD.—Potency I determine by experiment in my clinic, being governed by the favorable or unfavorable report of the patient. I find many of my students are prejudiced beforehand, and they soon learn to order the 30th cent. or higher.

Prof. ROYAL.—I do not teach potency, (and I detest the word,) because I do not know enough to teach it. I tell them what "attenuation" I use and explain it on the theory of individual susceptibility which varies in different persons and with different morbid conditions.

Prof. DEWEY.—I do not advocate any potency, believing that it is better to leave that to experience. I do mention the fact, however, that certain potencies of certain drugs, for instance the potencies of insoluble substances, act better. When asked by a student what potency of the drug it is better to commence practice with, I usually advocate the 3d and 6th unless it is some chronic case or in certain drugs where I advise the 30th and 200th dilution.

Prof. LEONARD.—I teach this under the head of dosage not as a personal opinion but from experience, occasionally detailing personal cases; but as far as obtainable I detail the usage of the profession. The usage of Hahnemann, Dunham, Hering and Hughes. Dosage is taught to be a strictly individual matter of experience, there being but few general principles as yet laid down except the Hahnemannian—the least medicine necessary to effect a cure. I do not attempt to explain the action of the dilution only on the general principle that in disease one is more susceptible to medicine than in health.

Prof. EDGERTON.—I do not teach potency.

Prof. PRICE.—I do not teach potency because it is a question as yet of individual experience, and the student should not be handicapped in the race by having his mind prejudiced at the start for or against any particular degree or subdivision of matter. Occasionally, however, I refer to some particular cure in my own experience, mentioning the dilution.

Prof. CHEESEMAN.—I do not teach the potency.

Prof. HAWKES.—I have deemed it better not to attempt to give arbitrary rules for the selection of the potency. I usually advise the students to carry several potencies from the highest to the lowest, and to test for themselves the efficacy of each, selecting for this purpose such cases as will not suffer to any considerable extent by waiting a sufficient time for such trial. I advocate in severe cases where the physician is in doubt as to which of several potencies would be best, to begin with a lower potency and follow it up at a reasonable interval of time with a higher one, believing that the patient should always have the benefit of the doubt.

Prof. ALLEN, H. C.—I never teach potency in any way. The potency is an unsettled question and I leave that to the experience of the student as illustrated in the clinic work of the college.

Prof. MONROE.--Not often taught. I explain that to obtain the primary action of a drug lower potencies are better; for its secondary action higher potencies. Some drugs have in my hands and in the hands of others failed in low potencies, others in high.

Dr. GRAMM.--In regard to the potency in homœopathic practice, the constitution age, sex and idiosyncrasy of the patient, and, also, the nature of the disease should decide. It is advisable to use the high and highest potencies with patients who are constitutionally weak, or have been weakened down by the sudden inroad and severity of the disease; or by its long standing without the proper treatment, particularly when the disease has become chronic, always cautioning against injudicious repetition. In acute diseases and naturally robust subjects, low potencies may cure, provided they are judiciously used so that undesirable aggravations are avoided.

Dr. PECK.--The potency of the remedy studied or prescribed should always be specified. The lecturer at the opening of his course, and the private instructor, at the first opportunity, should enunciate clearly the general principles of quantification in drug administration. Constitutional effects are more safely if not more promptly attained by the use of the higher than of the lower potencies. In every prescription the exact quantity of the selected substance should be specified and the determinative principles recited.

Dr. NIELSEN.—Yes, I would teach the potency. As I employ the lower potencies it is not very difficult for me to explain the therapeutic action of a remedy. In acute cases I employ and advocate the larger doses; in chronic cases the smaller; in the former because a decided and prompt action is required; in the latter cases smaller doses, because an insidious and gradual battle against the morbific factor is the most desirable.

Dr. KRAFT.--The potency question has been industriously skipped in class for fear of hurting some of the preconceived notions of the faculty or preceptor. The professor of therapeutics should be as much empowered to teach potency as is the surgeon to teach his especial technique in laparotomies, &c. If the technique does not conform to the ideas imbibed by the student or practitioner at a former period, or afterwards taken up, or if it is not borne out by the facts, then the student or practitioner should not be, as, of course, he is not, obliged to accept it. So also with the professor of therapeutics. His ideas of potency may not comform to those of the faculty, but if he adheres to the law of similars and the accredited authorities in Homœopathy of to-day he should not only be permitted but required to teach potency. He must give his reasons for so doing, however; it must not all be dicta. He must appeal to the judgment of the class, not to the precedent of his preceptor or his own experience solely. Hahnemann lays down certain rules for the profession in this regard, which if carefully studied and followed would very soon solve this vexatious and troublous question. There is a middle ground that is always safe in potencies as in other things; there need be no resort to the extremes of fad-ism.

Dr. BOJANUS—If we had settled rules for the prescription of different potencies or dilutions and knew for certain which cases of sickness correspond to the lower, middling, higher and highest potencies, question four might be answered by saying: that the student must be made acquainted with these rules and admonished to keep them. But as this, unfortunately, is not the case, the homœopathic student must be given the free choice of the potency, with the strict injunction, however, of keeping to small doses. Let him decide of this trifle according to his own sense, judgment and personal conviction.

Question 5.

When should the Organon be taught and how?

Answers.

Dr. DUDGEON.—The *Organon* being the best exposition of the homœopathic system, should be carefully studied by every one for himself, and its teachings accepted and endorsed by every teacher of Homœopathy when they are not inconsistent with the ascertained facts of modern science.

Dr. HUGHES.—The teaching of the *Organon* does not seem to me to belong to the chair of Materia Medica, but rather to that of Theory and Practice of Medicine. From this I would have it at some time in every student's course, read and critically commented on. I recommend Dr. Dudgeon's latest translation.

Dr. SKINNER.—The *Organon*, in my estimation, should be studied from the very first. In fact, I do not believe it possible for any man to have any sound conception of what Homœopathy is until he thoroughly understands and can take into his comprehension the vast and important tenets and truths of the greatest work that ever was published in Medicine, theoretically, doctrinally or practically.

Dr. BLAKE.—The *Organon* should be assimilated late in life probably.

Prof. MOHR.—The *Organon* should be studied during the first year so effectually that its great or fundamental principles will be indelibly fixed on the mind of the student. In the class-room, in the clinic and at every opportunity its practical rules should be brought to the attention of the students, for they cannot be too often repeated.

Prof. DEWEY.—The *Organon* should be taught during the second and third years of college course. And I believe in each homœopathic college a separate chair should be made for the *Organon* and *Institutes of Homœopathy*. Of course much of it can be taught in conjunction with lectures upon Materia Medica; but as it contains the philosophy of Homœopathy it seems to me that a separate chair for it is preferable, and it should be a chair insisted on by the American Institute, with two lectures a week at least.

Prof. HINSDALE.—The principles of homœopathy should be taught to freshmen, well grounding them in the philosophy of the theory of homœopathy. The *Organon* can be taught by class-room readings, preferably by seniors. Comments can be made as the reading advances and papers prepared by the students upon topics suggested by the author. The teaching of this valuable book should be critical and impartial. Adoration for Hahnemann should give place to admiration for the truth to be taught.

Prof. MCELWEE.—The *Organon* should be taught when the student's mind is rested and fresh; consequently the first thing in the morning, one or two paragraphs only at a time, those paragraphs being read by the student, who gives his idea of it, and then later, under the supervision of the professor, discusses it before the class.

Prof. GILMAN.—The *Organon* should be taught early and continually until it is mastered. It is the mother's milk to the medical student. It should be taught as the Bible is expounded—text by text, and explained and illustrated.

Prof. SNOW.—The *Organon* should be systematically taught during the first year of college, as it is the foundation work of Homœopathy. Frequent reference should be made to it, however, during the whole three years as occasion may demand. It should be committed to memory as nearly as possible, so that its precepts may remain always engraven on the mind.

Prof. MACK.—I do not use the *Organon* as a text-book. I think that one can better teach Homœopathy without the *Organon* as a text-book than with it.

Prof. COWPERTHWAITE.—The *Organon* should be taught by a separate teacher. It has not fallen to my lot to teach the *Organon* to any extent and I do not consider myself a competent judge as to how it should be taught. My method is to take my old and much loved copy which I held in my hand when I attended the lectures by Dr. Hering, and which is profusely filled with annotations, comments and underlinings according to Dr. Hering's suggestions. From this book I talk to the class, giving them Hahnemann's ideas, Hering's comments and my own views on each particular section as we take it up.

Prof. WOODWARD.—The *Organon* should be taught to beginners, not without judicious criticism.

Prof. ROYAL.—The *Organon* should be studied and taught throughout the entire student's course.

Prof. LEONARD.—For six years I have tried to teach the *Organon* in connection with Materia Medica and therapeutics; but whether from my own inability to do it well or from an incongruity of subjects, the results have not been satisfactory. A critical analysis of the *Organon*, with an exposition of its essential parts before senior students, seems to me to be part of the work of the chair of Theory and Practice, and it is so taught in the University of Minnesota.

Prof. EDGERTON.—The *Organon* should be taught to first course students. A text-book should be gotten up containing the essentials, and the student should commit the same to memory and recite in class.

Prof. PRICE.—In my opinion the *Organon* should be taught from the chair of Institutes, first omitting the psoric theory, dynamization, primary and secondary drug action, alternating drug effects, etc. There is too much difference of opinion upon these subjects amongst the best minds in our profession to make a belief in them a point of vital necessity. Of course the chair of Materia Medica and Therapeutics should teach the fundamental principles of Homœopathy whether the *Organon* be quoted or not.

Prof. CHEESEMAN.—The *Organon* should be taught by at least two lectures each week during the entire college course by a competent lecturer.

Prof. HAWKES.—The *Organon* should be taught from the "cradle to the grave" of medicine. In my judgment it should be taught as the good preacher teaches his congregation: select a portion for a text (and each section of the *Organon* is a sermon in itself) and elaborate to the student and explain its philosophy. Then make him explain it to me.

Prof. ALLEN, H. C.—The *Organon* should be taught every year of the entire course and taught by one who practices what he preaches. It is the foundation of our system, and no student can ever practice Homœopathy who does not know, and know most thoroughly, its principles.

Prof. PEMBERTON DUDLEY.—I hold to the view that every student should, first of all, be made acquainted with the methods—perhaps in

courtesy I should say "principles"—on which unhomœopathic treatment is applied to diseases and injuries by the various sects of physicians, and that his induction into the mysteries of Homœopathy should
come later. I am quite sure that the uncompromising adhesion to the
homœopathic law manifested by the "Homœopathic Fathers" was due
to the fact that they knew from both study and experience all about
allopathic methods and what these methods could and could not do for
their patients; and holding this view it would naturally follow that the
way to make staunch as well as intelligent homœopathists is to make
them quite fully acquainted with the effects and defects of the other
modes of medical practice first of all.

Having accomplished this we proceed as follows: We endeavor to
discover how the phenomenon known as "cure" is to be investigated.
(The allopath never concerns himself on this matter save only as to the
fact of its occurrence and the nature of the agencies by which it seems
to be brought about. The phenomenon does not present itself to his
mind as at all requiring investigation). This study forces us to the bedside as the only place where our curative studies can be pursued--the
only "laboratory" where principle of cure can be made known. Then
having learned the reasonableness and practicability of this method *of
finding out how to find out cures* for diseases, we turn to the *Organon* and
there discover that the author of that book has been before us and has
made the way plain for us. So we take up point after point in the development of curative science--first reasoning it out as well as we can,
and then turning to the book to find it all in Hahnemann's own words.
One of the things that our students discover and often mention in this
course is that the author of the *Organon* was anything but the dreaming
visionary he has been so often represented to be. In these studies of
Homœopathy both the student and the teacher are expected to have the
open book before them. In last winter's class of about eighty first-year
men I have counted over seventy copies of the *Organon* in the room at
one time, and all of them in use. We call it our "Sunday School Class
in the *Organon*."

Prof. MONROE.—It is a question in my mind whether the *Organon* should be taught during the student years; that is systematically. It should be referred to by the professor frequently, and the student should be taught that he cannot regard himself as a well-rounded homœopathic physician until he is familiar with the *Organon*. To my mind, however, the book is not of such a character as will admit of its being properly digested during the rushing, cramming gallop that marks the career of a student during his last year; and previous to that time, he is not sufficiently far advanced to comprehend it.

Dr. GRAMM.—Hahnemann's *Organon* should be read thoroughly by every student before entering a homœopathic college, and there it should be used by the regular professor of theory and practice as the foundation and guide for his teachings during all the four years. Every section should be properly read and carefully explained, and its teachings as much as possible illustrated by cases from actual practice from beginning to end.

Dr. PECK.—The *Organon* should be the first book placed in the hands of a medical student. If he has not sufficient sense and knowledge to understand and to appreciate it he never can become a trustworthy physician. The youth should be told to read it slowly and deliberately, stopping at any (to him) obscure point, or at any utterance that does not commend itself to his sober judgment and refer it at once to his instructor for their joint investigation. Rarely will this happen a half dozen times. One or two more rapid re-readings will do no harm. Since many alleged homoeopath physicians do not provide their pupils this instruction it becomes necessary for the college to teach the Institutes of Medicine. These should be taught at the very beginning instead of at the close of a course of study, for it is as important that a doctor should know what he believes, and why, as for the preacher, or any other man; and the sooner he ascertains this the better. After a little talk on Hahnemann and his times, display on the blackboard or in other

convenient manner singly and successively the various propositions. As
each is exhibited ask the class if it accepts that assertion, then call for
reasons *pro* and *con.*

Dr. NIELSEN.—The *Organon* should be taught especially to the advanced student, but by a competent teacher and one able to read between
the lines.

Dr. KRAFT.—The *Organon*, like the bible, should be read through not
less than once a year; its reading and study should not cease with the
medical man's commencement exercises. During school-life it should
be listened to from the chair of therapeutics at least once a week. Not
read by the teacher but talked. The professor of therapeutics should
have naught to do with Materia Medica; in him should be combined
the present highly ornamental chair of *Organon*, and the rare chair of
Institutes of Medicine. To him should be given the duties of explaining
the homœopathic law, the therapeutical application of Materia Medica,
the *Organon*, and the potencies.

Dr. BOJANUS.—Acccording to my opinion I should think that the
Organon should not be given before the end of the third year of study
and must be explained and commented in a special course of lectures,
and not before the students have visited the homœopathic and allopathic
clinics and hospitals for at least two years. In the lectures upon the
Organon, the whole homœopathic literature, with all its different ten-
dencies, must be passed in review and particular attention must be paid,
that the youthful students should not prefer the literature which has
given itself the task of clothing homœopathic therapeutics into a form
more or less like allopathy. Such compilations are a comfortable im-
plement in the hands of those who wish to convert science into a milk-
ing cow; they are useful to establish a position and keep their disciple
in the broad way of the beaten track, but this is preparing the ruin of
homœopathy.

Synopsis of Papers Presented.

What the Homœopath should know of Drugs.

By JABEZ P. DAKE, M.D., Nashville.

(Synopsis.)

The tendency has been to take too circumscribed a view of the part to be performed by the homœopathic practitioner. His duty is not simply to make drug comparisons. The homœopathic physician is called to poisoning cases as well as to self-limited and also fatal cases. In such events he must possess knowledge not circumscribed by his similia. The old school errs when it charges that the homoeopath cannot adopt other than his similia without becoming an allopath. The homoeopath is first a physician—an all-round, general physician.

He should know:

First. All the physical characteristics of the drugs he employs.

Second. Its poisonous properties and antidotes.

Third. Its pathogenetic effects.

Fourth. Its stimulant, anæsthetic, soporific or other palliative influence.

Drugs of any considerable power are all more or less poisonous, and it is not always easy to draw the line between the poisonous and the medicinal dose. The Materia Medica writer must cull from poisoning cases as well as from provings; thus getting both effects. It is important to get the facts and not the fancies. Applying all the rules of evidence to our Materia Medica, we realize that very few of the witnesses come up to the standard of the truth, the whole truth and nothing but the truth. Exhaustible provings there are none.

Wilson A. Smith, M.D., Chicago,

Professor of Materia Medica and Clinical Medicine in the
National Homœopathic Medical College,
Chicago.

The homoeopath looks forward to the time when his knowledge of drugs will be more complete, less vitiated, and more in keeping with the demands of Hahnemann's therapeutic law.

The homoeopath should be taught not only the symptomatology but as well the full nature of all drugs.

Discussion will be led by Dr. T. C. DUNCAN *of Chicago.*

The Indicated Remedy in Surgical Practice.

By HOWARD CRUTCHER, M.D., Chicago.

(*Synopsis.*)

In surgery, as in therapeutics, the problem always is upon the supplanting of pathology by physiology. Surgery is dependent upon the condition of the patient and not alone on the mechanical treatment given. Alarming hemorrhages in some cases defy the ordinary methods of control because a hemorrhagic diathesis taints the patient's tissues.

A case cited of the removal of a small lipoma in a practically bloodless locality, which nevertheless threatened to end the patient's life by hemorrhage. *Calcarea carb.* was seemingly indicated and arrested the bleeding. Yet *Calcarea carb* is not classed with hemorrhagic medicines.

Surgical patients prepared by homoeopathic remedies are better and safer patients to operate upon than those not so prepared.

Many surgical procedures are rendered unnecessary by the exhibition of the indicated remedy. Abscesses are prevented; hemorrhoids cured; bone diseases are healed, and numberless minor surgical conditions of the traditional school are cured. The case that will not respond to the indicated remedy is likely to prove a failure when subjected to operative measures; this is true especially of cancers. Reactive powers are measured by the indicated remedy.

(The indications for a number of remedies are then appended.)

A Study of Spigelia.

By S. F. SHANNON, M.D. Denver.

(*Synopsis.*)

This remedy was proved by Hahnemann, who recorded 525 symptoms in volume V. of his *Chronic Diseases.* Old school authorities say it is a most powerful anthelmintic, but that is all. They know nothing of its grand results in neuralgias, heart affections, or in nasal catarrh. Its chief action is on the nervous system--upon the nerves and their envelopes. Especially true is this of the nerves of special sense, and of its effects upon the fibrous and muscular tissue of the eyes, heart, and perhaps of the extremities. It is best indicated in light-haired, debilitated, pale, thin or bloated persons with great weakness. There is disinclination to work; restless and anxious; solicitous about the future; gloomy, suicidal.

A most peculiar characteristic of Spigelia is fear of pointed things, such as pins, scissors, needles.

Its headaches are worse from a jar like Belladonna or from noise or from thinking. The neuralgic headache begins in A. M., in cerebellum and extends over the left side of the head, causing violent, pulsating pains in left temple and over left eye. Anaemia of the optic nerve from excessive tea-drinking. This remedy should be remembered for anaemic, debilitated, subjects of rheumatic diathesis; for left-sided neuralgia, or for sick headaches; sun headaches; prosopalgia; rheumatic pericarditis, or endocarditis; rheumatic iritis; and mitral insufficiency.

(The whole paper is plentifully interwoven with valuable comparisons with other remedies.)

Discussion led by Dr. GEO. ROYAL *of Des Moines.*

The Picture seen from Different Standpoints.

By GEO. ROYAL, M.D., Des Moines.

(*Synopsis.*)

Dr. Ad. Lippe was opposed to pathology *per se*; yet in the introduction to his *Comparative Materia Medica* he gives a remedy for the gritting of the teeth when arising from intestinal disorders, but another remedy when it results from brain irritation. I take this as a good definition of pathology, namely: the knowledge of the cause of disease.

The student should be taught whether the remedy acts upon the brain or the stomach, whether upon the mucous membrane or the bones of the body; and he should know as far as possible the exact change produced on the tissues upon which the drug acts. The character of the pain differs as different tissues are affected. This will cause us to group our remedies.

I agree with Dr. T. F. Allen that had not our symptoms been arranged into a schema, the homœopathic Materia Medica would almost have died at its birth. Yet that method is to some most confusing. In Hering's *Condensed Materia Medica* the remedy Rhus has 975 odd symptoms; these are very confusing to the beginner, but when the symptoms are studied under their separate rubrics, then the pathological conditions appear. Thus by forming the symptoms into groups, the picture of septicæmia, of intermittent fever, of rheumatism, etc., appears.

Hering's *Condensed* should not be placed in the student's hands until he has been taught enough semiology to select groups of symptoms. Teaching of characteristic symptoms when isolated are objectionable for the same reason, and so also is the card system.

Dr. Royal cites a graphic case of the abuse of the card plan of studying Materia Medica.

The student should not only be taught that when a certain remedy is indicated all the symptoms are worse from wet weather, but *why* they are worse.

Materia Medica should be presented to the student in narrative form.

He should be taught to group drugs according to the tissues upon which they act; the different groups should be compared, placing particular stress on the mental symptoms and modalities in connection with the various dyscrasiæ. The student should be taught the semiology of the different dyscrasiæ. This was Boenninghausen's advice. The first two points will give you locations and sensations, and the last your conditions and modalities.

Discussion led by Dr. H. C. Allen *of Chicago.*

"And Therapeutics."

By T. C. Duncan, M.D., Chicago.

(*Synopsis.*)

Hahnemann did not have this appendix to his *Materia Medica Pura*, and were he here to-day he would condemn it. It is charged that the whole homœopathic profession does not study Materia Medica. How can they study it when its application (therapeutics) is made the chief study? The majority would say that the *Organon* explains the application of drugs; therefore it should be lectured upon. Therapeutics is field fighting; Materia Medica means drugs. Therapeutics belongs to Clinical Medicine. The old school has no Materia Medica, only therapeutic application.

Dr. Duncan reported an evening's visit with Father Hering in July, 1876, when Dunham, Allen, Raue, Farrington, Mohr, Lippe and Morgan were also present. On this occasion comparative Materia Medica was the evening's subject, and therapeutics was not once mentioned. In order to make it plain the title of Materia Medica might have added to it a sub-title and call it Drug Pathogenesy: Pathology and Symptomatology. Let us have a host of comparisons, a trained race of remedies as interesting as any other race, and one that will draw a crowd.

Discussion led by Dr. S. F. Shannon *of Denver.*

An Introduction to the Study of Natrum Muriaticum.

By SAMUEL A. JONES, M.D., Ann Arbor.

(Synopsis.)

Prof. Jones explains that during his professorship in the University of Michigan the use of "table salt"—and especially the thirtieth dilution thereof—in disease was a favorite theme for ridicule with both students and professors of "regular" dimensions. That salt had ever been used as a "remedy" in their own school was a therapeutical fact of which both professors and students were equally ignorant, and it was a double-barreled charity to enlighten them. Moreover, salt, says Prof. Jones, is indicated for dimness of sight and softening of the cartilages, and these symptoms occurring about that time, the first in some homœopathic students and the latter in the backbone of at least one homœpathic professor of that period, were "characteristics" that also called for the lecture.

The chloride of sodium plays an indispensible part in promoting the functions of the animal organism. Its importance in the metamorphosis of the tissues is shown by the fact that it forms the greater part of the soluble constituents of the ashes of all animal substances. It is found in the bile, blood, chyle, and in many exudations; in the gastric juice and the pancreatic; in the so-called muscular juice; in lymph, milk, saliva, sweat, tears, transudations, and in the urine. It is so uniformly present in vegetables that Lehman thought the ordinary article of food sufficient to supply the quantity of salt necessary for the animal body. Liebig shows that tempests carry salt from the ocean far into the interior, where they give it to spring water.

Prof. Foster says it aids in the metabolism of the body; that it preserves the form and color of the red-corpuscles. Vogel says it is absolutely necessary to the reproduction of many secretions. That an excess of salt may prove hurtful is evidenced by a lowering of the body temperature; in other words, by sub-oxidation. Boussingault experimented upon oxen. Those that were deprived of salt presented a less smooth and shining coat of hair, it being matted and in part fell off; their gait was heavy and they exhibited a cold temperament.

The quantity of an agent administered determines the quality of the result. Schussler says that salt acts on cartilaginous tissues, on mucous follicles and glands, and that it is indicated "in all catarrhs where the secretion is clear and transparent."

Pliny wrote that by nature salt is biting, hot and hurtful to the stomach; it moveth sweat and looseth the belly when taken in wine and water. The Code of Health of the school of Salernum says that the long protracted use of salt meats will hurt the sight, impair vitality and give rise to scab and cramps. Dr. Thomas Cogan in 1558, Dr. Thomas Venner in 1650, and Dr. Thomas Muffett in 1655 describe the evils of salt, very clearly giving the outlines of today's homœopathic provings.

Salt was used and is used today by the "regulars" in various forms of hemorrhages; it is in use by them for fevers of all kinds, in diarrhœas and dysenteries and in Asiatic cholera.

A number of interesting cases are cited to show the injurious effects of over-use of salt, and also the correction of such conditions by the use of the triturated salt.

If a disease continues whilst salt is taken daily in the patient's food, and if the same disease disappears when a trituration of salt is given, it must be evident that the triturated salt possesses qualities which are not found in the crude salt.

A case is given from an English homœopathic journal in which a clergyman's wife is relieved of a quinine hiccup with *natrum mur.* the 6th trit. Hence the triturated salt did what the crude salt was incapable of doing—curing a quinine hiccup. Especially as this lady had been eating salt daily in one and two teaspoonful doses. The Hahnemann method of preparing drugs for remedial purposes is not a mere dilution or attenuation, but a positively power-evolving or power-producing process, viz.: a true potentization or dynamization.

The Danger to Homœopathy.

By H. C. ALLEN, M.D., Chicago.

(Synopsis.)

An eloquent comparison is drawn between the principles involved in the signing of the Declaration of Independence and the principles contained in a proper knowledge and obedience to the tenets of Homœopathy. Our Materia Medica is the corner stone of our science and upon its correct teaching depends the success or failure of the individual practitioner; if that individual err in the application of remedial agents, failure more or less pronounced must be the inevitable result, and our system of therapeutics necessarily receives the blow. If similia be a law of nature it cannot be improved by a mixture with error.

Quotations are here made from Hering and Dunham to illustrate the danger of mixing allopathy with homœopathy in the hope of improving the latter.

Natural law is simplicity itself. The study of Materia Medica is not difficult if the law of Hahnemann be but followed implicitly. This keynote is found in paragraph 153 of the *Organon*, and when mastered, Homœopathy will no longer seem a bugbear to the student.

Method of Teaching Materia Medica.

By P. JOUSSET, M.D., Paris.

(Synopsis.)

There are two grand divisions in teaching Materia Medica: didactic and clinical. The first appertains to the professor, the second to the clinical application of his teachings.

Didactic teaching should follow the pathological lesions rather than the anatomical schema of Hahnemann.

It is necessary to distinguish between the effects obtained by toxic, medium and infinitessimal doses.

A medicine in a single dose produces two effects alternately opposite; again the same medicine will produce opposite effects according as it is given in strong or weak doses.

In the clinic it is necessary to establish comparisons between the actions of analogous medicines. It is important to specialize the indications for medicines designed for the heart, the stomach, the brain, the respiratory organs, &c.

In this department, also, we indicate the dose. The theoretical rule consists in applying to a class of symptoms the dose which reproduces these symptoms in the healthy man: *i. e.*, if we wish to contend against cardiac asystole we give a dose of digitalis which in a well man produces asystole. If we have to combat a heart trouble characterized by the energy of the throbbing, causing an increase of the arterial pressure, we give a weak dose, because the dose produces in the physiological condition the symptoms which we wish to combat.

In palliative medication the dose should always be strong; thus a strong dose of opium produces a cessation of pain; a strong dose of an emetic produces vomiting, &c.

If the theoretical study of Materia Medica makes the savant, its practical study makes the physician.

The Old-fashioned Way.

By WILSON A. SMITH, M.D., Morgan Park, Ill.

(*Synopsis.*)

In these days, when surgeons are made faster than the supply of surgical patients, a word favorable to Materia Medica will be appreciated. There is more occasion for felicitation over the practitioner who simply cures than he who must cut before he can attain his cure. The recent graduate as well as many older doctors regard humanity—especially female humanity—as so many anatomical specimens for the exercise of their mechanical skill. The appendix vermiformis is a normal growth from the beginning of Mosaic creation, and the indiscriminate taking out of this anatomical structure should be condemned. The same in relation to the ovaries of the woman. Instead of these manifold operations let us return to the beauty of homœopathic prescribing and cure our cases; for even when the man of knives and saws gets through with his work he is at sea if he cannot prescribe for his mutilated patient. Materia Medica studies should be made attractive; give the student the why and wherefore.

(The value of *nux vomica* and *pulsatilla* are then elaborated at some length in their curative relation to conditions which are commonly deemed as calling for the surgeon's knife.)

Notes.

The name of Dr. THEO. NIELSEN was inadvertently omitted from the table of contributors, in the early pages of this program.

Neither the portrait nor the revised paper of Prof. William Boericke, of the San Francisco Homœopathic School was received in time for the printers.

But one homœopathic school of the entire circle fails to appear in these pages by paper or portrait. Every effort was made to enlist its aid but without avail.

Mellins' Food. A good substitute for tea or coffee. Try it for your next patient.

American Institute members traveling via Chicago are cordially invited to visit The McIntosh Battery & Optical Co., 521 to 531 Wabash Ave.

Engelbach has the southern depot (New Orleans) for Homœopathic sundries.

Peroxide of Hydrogen should not lose its power by accidental or purposed uncorking. That's the kind handled by the Oakland Chemical Co.

The Windsor Hotel (Denver) is *first-class* in every particular, with reasonable charges.

The Minneapolis Pharmacy are also publishers of *The Minneapolis Homœopathic Monthly*.

Prof. J. C. Wood's new book on GYNECOLOGY is winning many praises for excellence of matter and diction. Boericke & Tafel never fail of issuing only first-class books. True also of their medicines.

www.ingramcontent.com/pod-product-compliance
Lightning Source LLC
Chambersburg PA
CBHW032355280326
41935CB00008B/587

*9 7 8 3 3 3 7 2 5 5 6 7 1 *